Flavo

THAME

GN00771046

RECIPES

Compiled by Julia Skinner

THE FRANCIS FRITH COLLECTION

www.francisfrith.com

First published in the United Kingdom in 2011 by The Francis Frith Collection®

This edition published exclusively for Identity Books in 2011 ISBN 978-1-84589-565-5

British Library Cataloguing in Publication Data

Flavours of ... Thames Valley - Recipes
Compiled by Julia Skinner

The Francis Frith Collection
Unit 6, Oakley Business Park,
Wylye Road, Dinton,
Wiltshire SP3 5EU
Tel: +44 (0) 1722 716 376
Email: info@francisfrith.co.uk
www.francisfrith.com

Printed and bound in Malaysia

Front Cover: **BRAY, THE LANDING PLACE 1899** 23621p

The colour-tinting is for illustrative purposes only, and is not intended to be historically accurate

CONTENTS

RECIPE

BROWN WINDSOR SOUP

Windsor, which lies beside the River Thames in Berkshire, is famous for its great castle, a favourite home of the Royal Family. It is the largest castle in England. Much of the castle that is visible from the river was built in the reign of George IV (1820-30), but the oldest parts of the castle, including the Round Tower, date from the 12th century. This was a favourite soup in Victorian times, and is said to have been served regularly at state banquets at Windsor Castle.

350g/12oz lean stewing steak, cut into cubes
25g/1oz butter
1 leek, the green part only, washed, trimmed and
   chopped into small pieces
1 onion, finely chopped
1 carrot, chopped into small pieces
1 tablespoonful plain flour
1.5 litres/ 2½ pints good beef stock
1 bouquet garni
Salt and pepper
Chopped fresh parsley, to garnish

Melt the butter in a large, heavy saucepan, and cook the onion for 2 minutes, then add the chopped leek and carrot, cover the pan with its lid and allow the vegetables to 'sweat' for 5 minutes. Add the beef, and stir until the cubes of meat are browned on all sides. Add the flour to a small amount of the stock to make a paste, then stir this into the pan, and gradually add the rest of the stock, stirring so that no lumps are formed. Bring everything to the boil, add the bouquet garni, salt and pepper to taste, cover and simmer gently for 2 hours. Remove the pan from the heat and allow the soup to cool a little.

Flavours of …
THAMES VALLEY
SOUP

Remove the bouquet garni. Liquidize the soup by pushing it through a sieve or processing it in a blender, test for seasoning and reheat before serving, garnished with chopped fresh parsley.

Some versions of this recipe have the soup served with a spoonful of cooked long-grain rice added to each bowl as an extra garnish.

READING, ON THE THAMES 1913 65921

The River Thames flows generally eastwards for a total of about 215 miles from its source in the Cotswolds, a few miles south of Cirencester in Gloucestershire, until it empties into the North Sea at the Thames estuary east of London; this book focuses on the centre section of the river as it winds through Oxfordshire, Berkshire and Buckinghamshire towards London and the sea – the area usually referred to as the Thames Valley. The area covered by the book also climbs onto the Chiltern Hills, and visits some of the towns and villages along various tributaries of the Thames.

WINDSOR, THE CASTLE 1914 66977

RECIPE

TROUT WITH ALMONDS

The River Thames at Marlow in Buckinghamshire was a favourite haunt of the 17th-century writer Izaak Walton, famous for his book 'The Compleat Angler', which is recalled nowadays in the name of the Compleat Angler Hotel in the town. Inside the hotel, some of the windows feature painted panels of the various fish that Izaak Walton described in his work. Apart from the Thames itself, its many tributaries that flow through Oxfordshire, such as the Cherwell, the Evenlode, the Windrush and the Ock, have always provided good fishing. During the Middle Ages it was said that salmon were so plentiful here that they formed a regular part of even the poorest person's diet! However, in modern times a catch of fish such as roach, bream and trout is more likely. This is a popular Oxfordshire way of cooking trout. The recipe will feed four people, so increase the quantities for more.

> 4 whole trout, gutted and cleaned, with the heads left on
> 4 tablespoonfuls plain flour
> Salt and pepper
> 115g/4oz butter
> 50g/2oz flaked almonds
> Juice of half a lemon
> Cut the remaining half of the lemon into thin slices, to garnish

Mix the flour with salt and pepper and use it to coat the fish on both sides. Melt 75g/3oz of the butter in a large frying pan. Slide in the trout and cook for about 15 minutes, turning halfway through cooking time, until they are golden brown on both sides and cooked through. Drain the trout and keep warm on a serving dish. Clean the pan, then melt the remaining butter in it. Add the flaked almonds and fry carefully until they are lightly browned, stirring frequently. Stir in the lemon juice and heat gently, then pour the sauce over the trout in the serving dish. Garnish with the lemon slices and serve.

MARLOW, FROM THE LOCK 1901 47125

ABINGDON
THE MARKET PLACE 1890
26994

RECIPE

FRIED EELS

Eels from the Thames have long been famous for their flavour, but the eels caught in the Abingdon area are particularly renowned for their good quality. Eels were eaten much more commonly in the past than they are nowadays, and were caught either in eel traps (long willow baskets) or with eel spears (slender forks shaped like a hand with metal fingers fixed to a long handle). In areas of England where eels were plentiful, they were often used as a currency in medieval times – for instance, the miller from the flour mill at Eynsham paid an annual rent of ten shillings and several hundred eels to his landlord, Abingdon Abbey.

> 450g/1 lb of skinned eels
> 50g/2oz seasoned plain flour
> 1 beaten egg
> 25g/1oz dry breadcrumbs
> Oil or butter for frying
> Finely chopped fresh parsley to garnish

Wash the eels, cut them into pieces about 8cm (3 inches) long, trim, and wipe them dry. Toss the pieces in the seasoned flour, then brush them with beaten egg, and roll them in the breadcrumbs until they are coated.

Heat the oil or butter in a frying pan until it is very hot, then add the eel pieces, a few at a time, and fry them until they are nicely browned and crispy. Remove from the pan and keep warm in a serving dish. Lightly fry the chopped parsley in the remaining oil or butter in the pan for a few seconds, then use it to garnish the eel pieces and serve.

MAIDENHEAD, HIGH STREET 1911 63797

RECIPE

BERKSHIRE HOG

Berkshire is famous for the quality of its pork. A local breed of pig is the Berkshire Pig, which was developed in the Thames Valley in the 18th century. It declined in popularity in the 20th century because the breed is slow-maturing and the meat was not lean enough for modern tastes, but in recent years there has been renewed interest in the Berkshire Pig and its fine, well-flavoured meat. This is the pork to seek out at good butchers and farmers' markets if you want to serve up a joint of roast pork with proper crispy crackling – you need that old-fashioned layer of fat on the meat to make really good crackling.

4 pork chops, wiped and trimmed
300ml/ ½ pint white wine or good stock
150ml/ ¼ pint single cream
115g/4oz mushrooms, wiped and sliced
1 tablespoonful oil
25g/1oz butter
8 shallots or very small onions, peeled
1 bouquet garni
1 tablespoonful plain flour
Salt and freshly ground black pepper

Heat the butter and oil in a frying pan. Add the pork chops and lightly brown them on each side. Remove the pork chops, add the sliced onions to the pan and gently cook until golden. Add the wine or stock and the bouquet garni. Return the pork chops to the frying pan, bring the liquid to the boil, cover and simmer gently for 45-60 minutes. Add the sliced mushrooms and cook for 10 minutes. Mix the flour with a little of the cream. Remove the pan from the heat and carefully stir in the flour and cream mixture. Return the pan to the heat, bring to the boil and boil for one minute, stirring all the time. Add the remainder of the cream, stirring well to heat through, but do not allow the sauce to boil. Remove the bouquet garni, adjust the seasoning and serve.

READING, THE MAIWAND MEMORIAL 1890 27139

'Bucks bread and beef' was an old saying reflecting the fact that Buckinghamshire supplied a good deal of both butter and cattle for the London market. Aylesbury, Buckinghamshire's county town, is located near the source of the River Thame (pronounced 'Tame'), which joins the Thames near Dorchester, between Oxford and Wallingford. This ancient hill town derived much of its wealth in the past from agriculture in the improved rich soils of the Vale of Aylesbury, and success in enterprises such as corn growing and duck rearing. The photograph below shows a livestock sale in Aylesbury's Market Square in 1921, the sheep penned and the cattle tied to improvised rails. The last livestock market in the square took place a few years later, in 1927.

AYLESBURY, MARKET SQUARE 1921 70551

RECIPE

BUCKINGHAMSHIRE BEEF BRAISED IN BEER WITH HERB DUMPLINGS

For the stew:
25g/1oz butter
2 tablespoonfuls oil
115g/4oz streaky bacon, chopped into small pieces
900g/2 lbs braising steak, cut into chunks
3 tablespoonfuls plain flour
450ml/ ¾ pint beer
450ml/ ¾ pint beef stock
1 bouquet garni
8 shallots or very small onions
175g/6oz button mushrooms

Salt & freshly ground black pepper

For the dumplings:
115g/4oz self-raising flour
50g/2oz shredded suet
Half a teaspoonful salt
Half a teaspoonful mustard powder
1 tablespoonful chopped fresh parsley
1 tablespoonful chopped fresh thyme

Melt half the butter with half the oil in a large heavy frying pan. Add the bacon pieces and brown on both sides, then transfer to a casserole dish. Brown the meat chunks in the frying pan in batches, transferring them to the casserole when browned. Stir the flour into the remaining fat in the pan. Gradually add the beer and stock, stirring continually to mix it well together. Season to taste, then bring to the boil, constantly stirring as it thickens. Pour the sauce over the meat in the casserole dish and add the bouquet garni. Cover the dish with its lid, and place in a cold oven. Set the oven temperature to 200°C/400°F/Gas Mark 6. Cook for 30 minutes, then reduce the temperature to 160°C/325°F/Gas Mark 3 and cook for a further 1 hour.

Heat the remaining butter and oil in a frying pan and cook the shallots or onions until they are golden. Take the onions out of the pan, add the mushrooms and cook quickly for 2-3 minutes. Add the onions and mushrooms to the casserole dish and cook for a further 30 minutes, then make the dumplings. Mix together the dumpling ingredients in a bowl, then add enough cold water to form a soft dough. Flour your hands and roll the mixture into about 12 balls, and place them on top of the stew. Replace the casserole lid and cook the stew for 25-30 minutes more, then serve.

Flavours of ...
THAMES VALLEY
MEAT, POULTRY AND GAME

RECIPE

BRAISED LIVER WITH NUTS AND RAISINS

This recipe comes from Marlow, in Buckinghamshire. It is an unusual but very tasty dish. Lamb or calf liver is best to use, as it has a more delicate flavour than pork liver.

750g/1½ lbs liver
50g/2oz butter
2 onions, peeled and finely sliced
25g/1oz plain flour
50g/2oz raisins
Half a teaspoonful dried chopped thyme
150ml/ ¼ pint red wine
600ml/1 pint beef stock
Salt and freshly ground black pepper
75g/3oz blanched almonds, coarsely chopped

Pre-heat the oven to 180°C/350°F/Gas Mark 4. Melt half the butter in a frying pan, add the sliced onions and cook them gently until they are soft and transparent – do not allow them to brown. Grease a wide, shallow casserole dish. Cut the liver into slices about 1cm (½ inch) thick and dip the slices in the flour to coat all sides. Place half the floured liver slices in the casserole, and cover with the cooked onions. Sprinkle half the raisins on top, and then sprinkle over the thyme. Place the remaining liver over this, and top with the remaining raisins. Mix the wine with the stock, salt and pepper, and pour it into the casserole. Cover the casserole with a piece of foil, and then the casserole lid. Cook in the pre-heated oven for 1¼ hours. Whilst the dish is cooking, fry the chopped almonds in the remaining butter until they are golden brown, but not burnt. At the end of the cooking time remove the casserole from the oven, uncover and sprinkle the fried almonds on top of the liver. Return the casserole to the oven, uncovered, for a further 5 minutes before serving.

WOOBURN, THE VILLAGE 1910 62231

RECIPE

BUCKINGHAMSHIRE LITTLE MUTTON PIES

This is a good way of using up cold lamb and potatoes leftover from the Sunday roast.

<u>For the filling:</u>
225g/8oz cold cooked lamb – or mutton if you can get it.
115g/4oz cold cooked potatoes
1 small onion
1 tablespoonful chopped fresh parsley
Half a teaspoonful finely chopped sage or rosemary
   (or mixed herbs if preferred)
Salt and pepper
A small amount of gravy or stock, to moisten
1 egg, beaten, to glaze
<u>For the shortcrust pastry:</u>
225g/8oz plain flour
50g/2oz margarine
50g/2oz lard
Half a teaspoonful of salt
2 tablespoonfuls of water

Pre-heat the oven to 220°C/425°F/Gas Mark 7.

To make the pastry, rub the fats into the flour until the mixture resembles fine breadcrumbs, then add just enough water to mix it all to a firm dough. Knead the dough lightly until it becomes smooth and pliable. Roll out the dough on a lightly floured surface and use it to line greased patty tins, reserving enough pastry to make lids for the pies.

Cut the meat and potatoes into small pieces, and finely chop the peeled onion. Mix together the meat, potatoes, onion, herbs and seasoning, adding a small amount of gravy or stock to moisten the mixture. Spoon the meat mixture into the pastry-lined patty tins. Roll out the reserved pastry and cut it into enough rounds to make a lid for each pie. Dampen the edges of the pastry and cover each pie with its lid, pressing the pastry edges firmly together to seal. Brush with the beaten egg, to glaze. Bake in the pre-heated oven for 15-20 minutes, until the pastry is crisp and golden.

RECIPE

DUCK BREASTS WITH PORT AND CHERRY SAUCE

A distinctive breed of duck was developed in the Aylesbury area of Buckinghamshire in the 18th century for the London meat market. Huge numbers of Aylesbury ducks were bred by 'duckers' in Aylesbury and the surrounding villages right up to the early 20th century, but most commercial breeders nowadays use hybrids, and the true Aylesbury duck breed is virtually extinct. This recipe celebrates the place of both ducks and cherries in Buckinghamshire's food history (for cherries, see page 46) – a good combination, as the slight acidity of the fruit cuts through the richness of the meat. Serves 4.

> 4 duck breasts
> Salt and freshly ground black pepper
> 300ml/10 fl oz good quality chicken stock
> 300ml/10 fl oz port
> 200g/7oz fresh cherries, pitted and halved
>   (or tinned cherries, well drained)
> 50g/2oz butter, cut into small pieces

Put the stock and port into a saucepan and bring to the boil. Let it bubble and reduce down for 15 minutes. Add the cherries, reduce heat and simmer for 10 minutes. Remove from the heat and put aside. Pat the skin of the duck dry with kitchen paper. Use a sharp knife to score the skin, then rub the portions with salt and pepper. Heat a heavy-based frying pan over a gentle heat, and place the duck in it, skin side down. Cook for 10 minutes until the skin is golden brown and crisp; then turn the duck over, increase the heat and cook the flesh side for 3-4 minutes. Remove the duck to a warm plate and leave to 'rest' for 5 minutes. Gently reheat the sauce. Add the pieces of butter to the sauce, one at a time, beating in each piece until it has melted before adding the next, to produce a rich, glossy sauce. Season the sauce to taste. Transfer the duck to warm serving plates, cut each portion into thick slices, spoon the sauce over them and serve with seasonal vegetables. A purée of celeriac or parsnips – or a combination of the two – is a good accompaniment to this dish.

RECIPE

RABBIT IN MUSTARD SAUCE

This recipe for a rabbit casserole with a rich, tasty sauce comes from Oxfordshire.

> 1 rabbit, jointed
> A dash of vinegar
> 115g/4oz streaky bacon rashers, rinds removed
> 4 onions, peeled and sliced
> A little fat or oil for frying
> 1 tablespoonful plain flour
> 450ml/ ¾ pint stock
> 150ml/ ¼ pint red wine
> 1 bouquet garni
> Salt and black pepper
> 1 teaspoonful made mustard
> 150ml/ ¼ pint of cream
> Chopped fresh parsley, to garnish

Soak the rabbit joints overnight in a bowl of salted water with a dash of vinegar in it, then drain, rinse and dry the rabbit. Cut the bacon rashers into small pieces. Heat some fat or oil in a flameproof casserole and fry the rabbit joints until they are browned on all sides. Remove the rabbit and keep to one side, then lightly fry the bacon pieces. When cooked, remove from the casserole and keep with the rabbit, then blend the flour into the fat in the casserole to make a roux. Gradually add the stock and the wine, a little at a time and stirring continuously so that no lumps are formed. Bring to the boil, stirring all the time, until the sauce thickens, then reduce heat to simmer. Add the salt, pepper and mustard to taste, then the rabbit, bacon, onion slices and bouquet garni. Cover with the casserole lid, and simmer very gently for about 1 hour, or until the rabbit is tender.

When cooked, remove the rabbit, place it on a serving dish and keep warm. Remove the bouquet garni, and if the sauce needs thickening reduce it by boiling rapidly. Remove the casserole from the heat, allow to cool for a few minutes, then stir in the cream. Warm the sauce through then serve the rabbit with the sauce spooned over, sprinkled with chopped fresh parsley.

COOKHAM MOOR, WAYFARERS 1890 27240

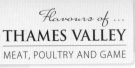

**MAIDENHEAD
BOATS IN BOULTERS
LOCK 1896** 37911x

RECIPE

DEVILLED CHICKEN LEGS

The photograph on the opposite page shows a variety of craft passing through Boulters Lock at Maidenhead in 1896, probably the most famous lock on the Thames. Many of these boats would be carrying a well-stocked picnic hamper to sustain their passengers during their day out. A Victorian picnic meant more than a plate of cucumber sandwiches: Mrs Beeton decreed that no self-respecting picnicker should venture out without a hamper overflowing with joints of cold roast beef, fowls, parcels of duck, ham, tongue, veal pie, pigeon pie, lobster, and a collared calf's head, to be followed by stewed fruit, cabinet pudding, jam puffs and plum pie – all home-made, of course. 'Devilling', or adding a mustard sauce to food, was very popular in Victorian times, and a recipe for Devilled Chicken Legs is given here. This hot, spicy dish could be eaten hot with strips of hot buttered toast, or eaten cold on picnics at regattas or boating trips on the Thames.

> 8 cooked chicken legs
> 2 teaspoonfuls of English mustard powder
> 1 teaspoonful of salt
> Half a teaspoonful of freshly ground black pepper
> Half a teaspoonful of cayenne pepper
> Half a teaspoonful of paprika
> 2 teaspoonfuls of mild curry powder
> 3 teaspoonfuls of French mustard
> 50g/2oz butter
> 1 tablespoonful of plain flour

Mix the mustard powder with half the salt, pepper, cayenne and paprika, the curry powder, and the French mustard, and work to a paste, then blend in half the butter. Make 4 slits down the length of each chicken leg and spread a little of the devil mixture into each. Season the flour with the remaining salt, pepper, cayenne and paprika. Use to dust the chicken legs. Melt the remaining butter and brush over each leg. Place under a pre-heated hot grill and cook for 6 minutes, turning to brown the legs on all sides. Baste with the pan juices once or twice.

HENLEY-ON-THAMES, THE REGATTA 1890 27200

OXFORD
CORNMARKET STREET
1922 71996

RECIPE

OXFORD JOHN STEAKS WITH CAPER SAUCE

'Oxford John' is a local name in Oxford for a lamb or mutton steak cut from the leg. The meat of an Oxford John is very tender and just needs gentle frying. It has long been a popular dish served at Oxford colleges, accompanied by a sharp, piquant sauce like caper sauce, which is a very traditional accompaniment to lamb and mutton in English cookery. If lamb leg steaks prove hard to find, lamb loin chops can be used instead. Serves 4.

> 4 lamb leg steaks (or loin chops),
>   each weighing 175g-200g (6-7oz)
> Salt and pepper
> 2 tablespoonfuls olive oil
> 25g/1oz butter
> 1 teaspoonful plain flour
> 300ml/ ½ pint good lamb or beef stock
> 1 tablespoonful of the vinegar from a jar of capers
> 2 tablespoonfuls drained capers

Season the lamb steaks with salt and pepper. Heat the olive oil and butter together in a heavy frying pan over a medium heat, and when the butter has melted, add the lamb steaks. Fry the steaks gently for 5-8 minutes on either side, depending on how pink you like your lamb, until they are browned on both sides. Remove the steaks from the pan and keep warm whilst you make the sauce. Add a dash of the stock to the pan to deglaze it, and stir the bottom of the pan with a wooden spoon to loosen any sediment. Stir in the flour and cook for 2 minutes, stirring all the time. Gradually add the stock, stirring continuously, bring to the boil and continue to cook for a further 3-4 minutes, stirring all the time, until the sauce has become thick and smooth. Stir in the vinegar and the capers, then reduce the heat and simmer for a further 2 minutes. Taste the sauce, and season as necessary. Return the lamb steaks to the pan and allow them to simmer in the sauce for 5 minutes. Serve immediately, whilst piping hot, with seasonal vegetables.

RECIPE

OXFORD SAUSAGES

Traditional Oxford Sausages are rather unusual, as they are not made in skins, and are made from equal quantities of minced pork and veal or lamb. They are delicious, and simple to make at home.

> 225g/8oz pork, minced or finely chopped
> 225g/8oz veal or lamb, minced or finely chopped
> 115g/4oz shredded suet
> 115g/4oz fresh breadcrumbs, moistened with water
> Grated zest of ¼ lemon
> Half a teaspoonful grated nutmeg
> Half a teaspoonful fresh chopped sage
> Half a teaspoonful dried mixed herbs
> 1 teaspoonful salt
> Half a teaspoonful freshly ground black pepper
> 1 egg, beaten
> A little plain flour for coating
> A little lard or oil for frying

Mix the meats, suet, breadcrumbs, lemon zest, nutmeg, herbs, salt and pepper in a large bowl. Add the egg to the mix and mix thoroughly. Flour your hands and form the mix into sausage shapes (or small flat cakes if preferred). Coat each sausage with flour.

Fry in a little lard or oil (or grill if preferred) for about 8 minutes, or until they are thoroughly cooked through.

DORCHESTER, THE VILLAGE 1890 27015

The source of the River Thame (pronounced 'Tame') is several streams which converge near Aylesbury in Buckinghamshire. The Thame then flows through farmland before reaching the town of Thame, then swings southward to Dorchester, about 8 miles south-east of Oxford, where it converges with the River Thames. Historically the Thames was only so-named downstream of Dorchester; upstream it was named the Isis, but this distinction is rarely used outside Oxford. This local name for the Thames has given its name to a rather special cheese made by The Oxford Cheese Company, which has a shop in Oxford's Covered Market. Oxford Isis is a full-fat soft cheese encased in a yellow rind that is washed with local honey mead before it is ripened, maturing to a creamy consistency with a distinctive flavour and aroma. Oxford Isis won the Cheese Lovers Trophy at the British Cheese Awards in 2009. Also made by The Oxford Cheese Company is the award-winning Oxford Blue, a full-flavoured blue-veined cheese with a creamy, smooth texture. Both cheeses are well worth seeking out in specialist cheese shops and fine food stores.

29

OXFORDSHIRE CARROT PUDDING

Carrot puddings often appeared in British recipe books of the 18th and 19th centuries, as well as puddings made from other sweet root vegetables, such as parsnips and pumpkins. This old Oxfordshire recipe makes a sweet pudding that is surprisingly tasty – it is well worth trying, and a good way of using up leftover pieces of bread. The flavour of the carrots combines very well with the nutmeg and cinnamon.

> 225g/8oz carrots
> A pinch of salt
> 115g/4oz butter or margarine, softened to room temperature
> 115g/4oz caster sugar
> 2 eggs, separated
> 225g/8oz fresh breadcrumbs (brown or white)
> 1 teaspoonful ground cinnamon
> ¼ teaspoonful freshly grated nutmeg (use more if you like it)

Wash and trim the carrots, cut them into slices and then cook them in a saucepan of boiling lightly salted water until they are tender. Drain the carrots, then push them through a sieve or liquidize them in a blender to make a purée. In a large bowl, cream together the sugar and butter or margarine until the mixture is light and fluffy. Beat the egg yolks into the mixture, then stir in the breadcrumbs until they are well mixed in. Add the carrot purée, cinnamon and nutmeg and combine it all together thoroughly. In another bowl, whisk the egg whites until the mixture is thick and glossy and can form peaks. Use a large metal spoon to carefully and gently fold the egg whites into the carrot mixture – take some time to do this properly, so that it is all well mixed together. Grease a 1.2 litre (2 pint) pudding basin, and fill it with the pudding mixture. Cover the pudding basin with its lid if you have one, otherwise make a lid of pleated greaseproof paper, and then another of pleated foil (this allows room for the pudding to expand during cooking), and tie down firmly with string. Place the pudding basin on a trivet or an upturned saucer in a large saucepan. Pour enough boiling water into the pan to come halfway up the sides of the basin. Place the pan on heat and bring the water back to the boil, then cover the pan with its lid and steam the pudding for about 2 hours, replenishing the pan with more boiling water when necessary, so that it does not boil dry. When cooked, turn out the pudding on to a warmed serving dish, and serve with custard or cream.

CLIFTON HAMPDEN, THE BARLEY MOW INN 1890 27010

WINDSOR, THE CASTLE FROM CLEWER PATH 1890 25607

RECIPE

POOR KNIGHTS OF WINDSOR

The Poor Knights was an order of military pensioners founded by Edward III in 1349 whose job it was to pray for the souls of the Knights of the Garter in return for relief and comfortable sustenance. It was Henry VIII's daughter, Queen Mary I, who reigned from 1553-1558, who was responsible for having a row of almshouses for the 'Poor Knights' built into the south wall of Windsor Castle. This simple recipe is a good way of using slightly stale, leftover bread to make a deliciously rich but economical dessert that belies its name. This makes enough for 4 people.

> 4 slices of stale white bread with their crusts removed
> 1 tablespoonful of caster sugar
> 150ml/5 fl oz milk
> 1 tablespoonful of sherry
> 4 egg yolks, beaten
> 75g/3oz butter
> 1 teaspoonful of ground cinnamon
> A red jam of choice – strawberry, raspberry, bramble, damson etc

Dissolve the sugar in the milk in a shallow dish, and add the sherry. Cut each slice of bread in half, and dip each half into the milk mixture, and then into the beaten egg yolks to coat them. Melt the butter in a wide frying pan, and fry the bread pieces a few at a time until they are golden brown on both sides.

Drain each piece as it has been cooked, and keep hot until all the slices have been fried.

Sprinkle the fried bread slices generously with sugar and cinnamon and serve whilst they are still hot, spread with jam.

RECIPE

ETON MESS

On the opposite bank of the River Thames from Windsor is Eton, famous for its public school. This utterly irresistible dessert comes from Eton College, where it is served to parents and pupils on the college lawns at the annual picnic and prize-giving day in the summer.

> 450g/1 lb fresh strawberries, chopped into pieces
> 4 tablespoonfuls of kirsch or elderflower cordial
> 300ml/ ½ pint double cream
> 6 small white meringues

Put the strawberries in a bowl, sprinkle over the kirsch or elderflower cordial, then cover and chill for 2-3 hours.

Whip the cream until soft peaks form, then use a large metal spoon to gently fold in the strawberries and their juices.

Crush the meringues into rough chunks, then scatter them over the strawberries, and gently fold them in so that everything mixes together.

Spoon the mixture into a serving dish, or into individual dishes, and serve as soon as possible.

ETON, ETON SCHOOLBOYS IN THE HIGH STREET 1906 56036A

WEST WYCOMBE, HIGH STREET 1906 53690

RECIPE

STONE CREAM

This is a very old recipe for a creamy dessert from Buckinghamshire.

> 4 tablespoonfuls of cold water
> 15g/½ oz gelatine
> Any jam, such as strawberry, raspberry or cherry
> The separated whites of 2 eggs
> 300ml/ ½ pint double cream
> 1 dessertspoonful of caster sugar
> A few drops of vanilla essence
> 300ml/ ½ pint milk

Put the water in a small bowl and add the gelatine. Place the bowl over a pan of hot (but not boiling) water, and stir gently until the gelatine has dissolved and it all becomes clear. Remove the pan from the heat and allow the mixture to cool for a few minutes, but not to become cold or it will set.

Put some jam in the bottom of a serving dish, or in individual glass sundae-type dishes. Whisk the egg whites until they form soft peaks. In a separate bowl whisk the cream to the same consistency as the egg whites, and fold in the sugar and a few drops of vanilla essence. Add the gelatine to the milk and then gently mix this into the cream mixture. When the mixture is beginning to thicken, fold in the whisked egg whites and straight away pour the mixture into the serving dish or dishes on top of the jam. Put the Stone Cream into the refrigerator until needed, covered with cling film, and serve chilled.

RECIPE

CHILTERN HILLS PUDDING

The River Wye rises in the Chiltern Hills of Buckinghamshire and flows for around 9 miles through the county down to Bourne End, where it meets the River Thames above Cookham Lock in Berkshire. High Wycombe takes part of its name from the river, which now runs mostly underground through the town.

> 4 level tablespoonfuls of tapioca
> 300ml/ ½ pint milk
> 115g/4oz raisins
> 25g/1oz shredded suet
> 115g/4oz sugar
> 115g/4oz fresh white breadcrumbs
> 1 level teaspoonful of bicarbonate of soda

Place the tapioca in a bowl, cover with the milk and leave it to soak for 2 hours, then strain off the milk and reserve it. Add the raisins, suet, sugar and breadcrumbs to the tapioca. Dissolve the bicarbonate of soda in the strained milk, then add it to the other ingredients and mix well together.

Put the mixture into a greased 1.2 litre (2 pint) pudding basin. Cover the basin with its lid, or with a lid made of pleated foil (to allow room for the pudding to rise), and tie it down firmly with string. Place the basin in a large saucepan half filled with boiling water, bring the water back to the boil, then cover the pan with its lid and steam the pudding for about 3 hours, replenishing the pan with more boiling water when necessary and taking care not to let the pan boil dry. Serve with cream or custard.

HIGH WYCOMBE, FROGMORE SQUARE 1921 70607

MAPLEDURHAM, THE MILL 1890 27091

RECIPE

HOLLYGOG PUDDING

This intriguingly-named pudding comes from Oxfordshire and is very easy to make. It is an old-fashioned rich, stodgy, roly-poly-type pudding with a golden crust that is partially cooked in milk. As it cooks, the syrup and milk form a delicious sweet sauce.

> 225g/8oz plain flour
> A pinch of salt
> 115g/4oz butter
> 300ml/10 fl oz full fat milk
> 4 tablespoonfuls of golden syrup
> 25g/1oz extra butter, cut into small pieces

Pre-heat the oven to 200°C/400°F/Gas Mark 6 and grease a deep ovenproof dish.

Sieve the flour and salt together into a large mixing bowl. Rub in the butter until the mixture resembles fine breadcrumbs, and mix in just enough of the milk to form a stiff dough. Gather the dough into a ball and knead it lightly for a minute or so, then roll out the dough on a lightly floured surface to form a long rectangle, about 5mm (¼ inch) thick. Spread the dough with the golden syrup, and roll it all up like a Swiss roll.

Place the roll in the greased ovenproof dish, seam side down, and pour the remaining milk into the dish – it should come to about halfway up the sides of the pudding. Dot the small pieces of the extra butter over the top of the pudding. Bake in the pre-heated oven for 30-40 minutes, until the pastry is golden brown and the sauce is bubbling.

RECIPE

OXFORD PUDDING

175g/6oz shortcrust pastry
350g/12oz fresh apricots (or canned apricots can be
   used if preferred, well drained and chopped)
115g/4oz caster sugar
2 eggs
2 tablespoonfuls double cream

Pre-heat the oven to 180°C/350°F/Gas Mark 6.

Cook the apricots in a small amount of water with half the
sugar until they are very soft, then remove the skin and stones
and chop the fruit into small pieces. Add a little more sugar to
taste, if necessary. Separate the eggs. Beat the egg yolks into
the cream and mix in with the fruit. Roll out the pastry on a
lightly floured board and use it to line a greased ovenproof
pie or flan dish. Fill with the fruit mixture, and bake in the pre-
heated oven until the filling is set.

Whisk the egg whites until soft peaks form, and fold in the
remaining sugar, to make a meringue mix. Remove the pie tin
from the oven, pile the meringue mixture on top of the pie
filling and shape it into peaks with a fork. Reduce the oven
temperature to 150°C/300°F/Gas Mark 2. Return the pie to the
oven and cook at the reduced heat for a further 20 minutes, or
until the meringue is cooked and golden brown. This can be
served hot or cold.

**OXFORD, TRAFFIC IN THE HIGH
STREET 1900** 45182x

BANBURY APPLE PIE

This apple pie from Banbury has a pastry base and a pastry lid, a style of pie sometimes called a 'plate pie'.

For the enriched pastry:
350g/12oz plain flour
A pinch of salt
175g/6oz butter or margarine
1 tablespoonful caster sugar
1 egg

For the pie filling:
675g/1½ lbs cooking apples
Juice of half a lemon
115g/4oz sultanas
Finely grated rind and juice of
    1 orange
75g/3oz soft light brown sugar
1 teaspoonful ground cinnamon
¼ teaspoonful freshly grated
    nutmeg
A little milk, to glaze
A little extra caster sugar for
    sprinkling

Pre-heat the oven to 200°C/400°F/Gas Mark 6 and grease a shallow pie dish, or pie plate. Put the flour and salt in a bowl and rub in the butter or margarine until the mixture resembles fine breadcrumbs, then stir in the tablespoonful of caster sugar. Beat the egg and stir it in, then add just enough cold water to bind the mixture together. Lightly knead the dough until it is smooth and elastic. Cut off two-thirds of the dough and roll it out to a round on a lightly floured surface, then use it to line the prepared pie dish or plate.

Peel and core the apples and cut them into thin slices, then sprinkle them with the lemon juice to prevent them discolouring. Layer the apple slices, sultanas, orange rind, soft brown sugar and spices in the pie dish, keeping the filling slightly domed in the centre, then drizzle the orange juice over it all. Brush round the upper rim of the pastry with water.

Roll out the remaining piece of pastry to form a lid for the pie. Brush the edge of the pastry with water, then lay it over the filling in the pie dish. Trim the two edges, then use the flat side of a knife blade to press down firmly all round the edges, to seal them together well and form a decorative rim. Cut a slit in the centre of the pastry lid to allow steam to escape during cooking. Brush the pie with milk to glaze, then bake in the pre-heated oven for 30-40 minutes, until the pastry is crisp and golden. Remove from the oven and sprinkle the top with a little caster sugar. This pie can be served hot or cold.

Ride a cock-horse to Banbury Cross
To see a fine lady upon a fine horse
With rings on her fingers and bells on her toes
She shall have music wherever she goes.

BANBURY, THE CROSS 1921 70582

Banbury in north Oxfordshire developed alongside the River Cherwell, a major tributary of the Thames. The town is famous for Banbury Cakes (see page 47), and its cross, linked with a well-known nursery rhyme. Banbury's medieval cross of the rhyme was destroyed in the 17th century and the town was without its famous symbol until the 1850s, when a replacement cross was erected. Most people are familiar with the first verse of the nursery rhyme, shown above, but there is a second verse, included in 'Tommy Thumb's Pretty Song Book' (c1744), which is not so well-known:

> *Ride a cock-horse to Banbury Cross*
> *To see what Tommy will buy.*
> *A penny white loaf, a penny white cake,*
> *And a two-penny apple pie.*

Unfortunately the Banbury apple pie on the opposite page will cost rather more than two pence to make nowadays!

RECIPES

BUCKINGHAMSHIRE CHERRY TURNOVERS
(OR BUMPERS)

Buckinghamshire used to be famous for its soft fruit, and especially for cherries; it was common to see livestock (including Aylesbury ducks) grazing beneath the trees in acres of cherry orchards. Local cherry varieties are the now-rare Stewkley Red and the jet-black Prestwood Black. Until fairly recent times the first Sunday in August was known in Buckinghamshire as 'Cherry Pie Sunday', when the completion of the cherry harvest with the gathering of the late Prestwood Blacks (known locally as 'chuggies') was celebrated with the eating of cherry pie or other delicacies such as cherry turnovers or cherry duff. In her book 'In Touch', published in 1961, Rita Allen described how the Plough Inn in the hamlet of Lower Cadsden celebrated Cherry Pie Sunday in the 1960s: 'A wooden counter is placed outside and is piled high with cherry turnovers brought from the inn table; over a thousand were made for the occasion last year (1960), and the crowds were waiting to sample them long before 7pm.'

> 450g/1 lb fresh cherries
> 75g/3oz soft brown or caster sugar
> 225g/8oz shortcrust pastry
> A little milk, to finish
> A little extra caster sugar, to finish

Pre-heat the oven to 200°C/400°F/Gas Mark 6. Grease a couple of baking trays and line with dampened greaseproof or baking paper. Stalk and stone the cherries. Roll out the pastry on a lightly floured surface and cut it into 10cm (4 inch) rounds – you can do this by cutting around a saucer. Heap the centre of each pastry round with cherries, leaving a good margin round the edge, and sprinkle liberally with sugar. Damp the edges of each pastry round by brushing it with water, then bring up one half of each round over the filling to the other side, to make a half-moon shape, like a pasty. Seal the edges well by pinching them together with your fingers, then crimp along the rounded edge with a fork. Brush each turnover with a little milk and sprinkle with a little caster sugar. Bake in the pre-heated oven for about 25 minutes. Place on a wire rack and dredge with more sugar. These can be eaten eat hot or cold.

BANBURY CAKES

These small pastry cakes from Banbury, made with puff or flaky pastry and filled with a spicy dried fruit mixture known as Banbury Meat, date back in various forms to at least Tudor times, although it is thought that they were produced earlier than that – the original Banbury Cake recipe is said to date from the 13th century, when crusaders brought back dried fruit and spices from the East. The use of rum in this recipe is an authentic touch, but can be omitted if preferred. Banbury Cakes are best eaten on the same day as they are made, otherwise the pastry can be 'refreshed' by reheating them gently in a low oven for 10 minutes. The traditional shape for Banbury Cakes is oval, not round.

500g/1 lb puff or flaky pastry
50g/2oz melted butter
175g/6oz currants, or a mixture of currants and raisins
50g/2oz mixed peel
½ teaspoonful ground allspice, or mixed spice if preferred
½ teaspoonful ground nutmeg
½ teaspoonful ground cinnamon
75g/3oz caster sugar
1 dessertspoonful of rum
1 egg white
A little extra caster sugar to finish

Pre-heat the oven to 220°C/425°F/Gas Mark 7. Grease 2 baking sheets and cover with greaseproof or baking paper. Roll out the pastry thinly on a lightly floured surface. Cut the dough into circles about 15cm (6 inches) in diameter – use a small plate or saucer to cut around. Mix together the melted butter, dried fruit and, spices, sugar and rum. Place a generous spoonful of the filling into the middle of each pastry circle and spread it evenly over the pastry, leaving a good margin around the edges. Dampen the edge of each pastry circle and draw up the sides over the filling to meet in the centre, as if you are making a small Cornish pasty. Pinch and crimp the edges firmly together, to seal them well. Turn each cake over so that the join is underneath, then gently form the cakes into an oval shape with your hands, then press down very lightly on each cake with a rolling pin, to flatten it slightly. When all the cakes are assembled, use a sharp knife to cut three diagonal slashes across the top of each one. Brush the cakes with egg white and dredge them with the extra caster sugar. Place the cakes on the prepared baking trays and bake in the pre-heated oven for 15-20 minutes, until they are risen and the pastry is golden brown.

RECIPE

BAMPTON PLUM CAKE

West of Oxford, Bampton stands on a small tributary of the infant River Thames. Bampton is famous for the Morris dancing which takes place through the village on the Monday of the Spring Bank Holiday in May. The dancing starts at 8.30 at the junction of Bushey Row and New Road, and then continues through the day at various locations in Bampton – including the pubs, of course. A plum cake skewered on a sword is carried by the dancers as they make their way round the village. Pieces of the cake are sold and are supposed to bring good luck to all who eat them. The cake is also known as a 'fertility cake', and ladies watching the dancing are warned that if they eat a piece of it they may have a baby with them by the same date next year! It is called plum cake because originally it would have been made with dried plums – or prunes – but it is usually made with raisins nowadays.

> 450g/1 lb self-raising flour
> 225/8oz butter or margarine
> 115g/4oz caster sugar
> 115g/4oz soft brown sugar
> 1 tablespoonful of black treacle
> 225g/8oz raisins
> 3 eggs, beaten
> Half a teaspoonful of vanilla essence
> A small amount of milk, to mix

Pre-heat the oven to 160°C/325°F/Gas Mark 3. Cream together the butter or margarine, sugar and treacle, until the mixture is light and fluffy. Gradually beat in the beaten eggs, a little at a time, until the mixture is well blended – add a little flour if necessary, to prevent the mixture from curdling – then stir in the raisins. Mix the vanilla essence with the milk. Fold the flour into the mixture, adding a little of the milk and vanilla essence, and mix it all together to make a soft dropping consistency. Line a 20cm (8 inch) cake tin with greaseproof paper, and spoon the mixture into the tin. Bake in the pre-heated oven for 2-2½ hours, until the cake is risen and firm to the touch.

BRACKNELL, HIGH STREET 1901 46894x

WARGRAVE, THE VILLAGE 1890 27177

RECIPE

SPICED APPLE CAKE

One of Britain's favourite apple varieties was developed at Colnbrook near Slough (then in Buckinghamshire but now in Berkshire) in the 1820s, when Richard Cox planted a seed from a Ribston Pippin which he pollinated with a Blenheim Orange. Cox's Orange Pippin is now the most important British dessert apple, accounting for three quarters of all dessert apples grown in the country. Either cooking apples or dessert apples can be used to make this cake – including Cox's Orange Pippins.

> 225g/8oz plain flour
> 2 teaspoonfuls baking powder
> 75g/3oz butter or margarine
> 75g/3oz soft brown or caster sugar
> 1 teaspoonful ground cinnamon
> 1 teaspoonful mixed spice
> 450g/1 lb apples (cooking or dessert apples, as preferred)
> 75g/3oz raisins or sultanas
> 1 egg, beaten
> 1-2 tablespoonfuls milk
> 25g/1oz soft brown or caster sugar for the topping
> ¼ teaspoonful ground cinnamon for the topping

Pre-heat the oven to 200°/400°F/Gas Mark 6. Grease a 20cm (8 inch) cake tin and line the base and sides with greaseproof or baking paper. Peel and core the apples and dice them into small pieces. Sift together the flour and baking powder into a large mixing bowl. Rub in the butter or margarine, then stir in the cinnamon and mixed spice, then the sugar, the apples, and the raisins or sultanas. Stir in the beaten egg, then mix in just 1-2 tablespoonfuls of milk – the mixture will seem quite chunky and dry, but this is correct. Give it all a good mix-up together, then pile the mixture into the cake tin and smooth the top. Mix together the sugar and cinnamon for the topping, and sprinkle it evenly over the cake mixture. Bake in the pre-heated oven for 45-50 minutes, until the cake is risen and firm to the touch. Remove from the oven and leave to cool in the tin for 10 minutes, then turn out on to a wire rack, carefully peel off the baking paper and leave to cool completely.

OXFORD MARMALADE TEABREAD

A famous food associated with Oxford is marmalade. Oxford marmalade is characteristically chunkier than most other marmalades, traditionally made with a high proportion of bitter Seville oranges and darkened with the addition of a little black treacle. The name that is most commonly associated with Oxford marmalade is that of Frank Cooper, but it was his wife Sarah-Jane who actually created the recipe for this marmalade. One day in 1874 Mrs Cooper made 76 pounds of her special marmalade and her husband Frank started selling it in his grocery shop at 83 High Street in Oxford. It became so popular that Frank eventually opened a factory in Oxford to make enough marmalade to cope with the demand. Although the commercial version of Frank Cooper's Oxford Marmalade is no longer made in Oxford, it remains part of the city's food history and heritage. This recipe uses Oxford marmalade to make a delicious teabread to serve cut into slices at teatime. The marmalade helps to keep it moist as well as giving it a lovely flavour. You can use either fine cut or chunky cut marmalade – whichever is your own preference for spreading on your breakfast toast!

> 200g/7oz plain flour
> 1 teaspoonful baking powder
> 1 heaped teaspoonful ground cinnamon
> 115g/4oz butter or margarine, cut into small pieces
> 50g/2oz soft brown sugar
> 4 tablespoonfuls Oxford orange marmalade
> 1 egg, beaten
> 3 tablespoonfuls milk

Pre-heat the oven to 160°C/325°F/Gas Mark 3. Grease a 1kg (2 lb) loaf tin, and line the base with greaseproof or baking paper. Sift the flour, baking powder and cinnamon together into a mixing bowl, add the butter or margarine and rub it in with your fingertips until the mixture resembles fine breadcrumbs, then stir in the sugar. In another bowl, mix together the marmalade, the beaten egg and milk, then stir this into the flour and mix thoroughly to make a soft, dropping consistency – add a little more milk if necessary. Turn the mixture into the prepared loaf tin, and bake in the pre-heated oven for 1¼ -1½ hours, until the surface of the cake is firm to the touch. Remove from the oven and leave to cool in the tin for 5 minutes, before turning out onto a wire rack and carefully peeling off the paper. Leave to cool completely. Serve cut into slices, buttered if liked.

NEWBURY, MARKET PLACE 1952 N61024

The Berkshire town of Newbury is sited beside the River Kennet, which meets the Thames at Reading. Speenhamland is a district to the north of the River Kennet, between the centre of Newbury and the village of Speen. The Pelican Inn at Speenhamland was the setting in 1795 for a meeting of Berkshire magistrates which has gone down in history as the introduction of the infamous Speenhamland System. This was a way of calculating the amount of relief that should be paid to the poor from the local parish rates by tying the amount of relief payments to the cost of a loaf of bread, according to family size and the level of local wages. The Speenhamland System came to be used all over England, but was much criticised as it resulted in employers deliberately keeping wages at a low level, knowing that the difference would be made up by people being forced to undergo the humiliation of applying for assistance from the parish.

FRANCIS FRITH

PIONEER VICTORIAN PHOTOGRAPHER

Francis Frith, founder of the world-famous photographic archive, was a complex and multi-talented man. A devout Quaker and a highly successful Victorian businessman, he was philosophical by nature and pioneering in outlook. By 1855 he had already established a wholesale grocery business in Liverpool, and sold it for the astonishing sum of £200,000, which is the equivalent today of over £15,000,000. Now in his thirties, and captivated by the new science of photography, Frith set out on a series of pioneering journeys up the Nile and to the Near East.

INTRIGUE AND EXPLORATION

He was the first photographer to venture beyond the sixth cataract of the Nile. Africa was still the mysterious 'Dark Continent', and Stanley and Livingstone's historic meeting was a decade into the future. The conditions for picture taking confound belief. He laboured for hours in his wicker dark-room in the sweltering heat of the desert, while the volatile chemicals fizzed dangerously in their trays. Back in London he exhibited his photographs and was 'rapturously cheered' by members of the Royal Society. His reputation as a photographer was made overnight.

VENTURE OF A LIFE-TIME

By the 1870s the railways had threaded their way across the country, and Bank Holidays and half-day Saturdays had been made obligatory by Act of Parliament. All of a sudden the working man and his family were able to enjoy days out, take holidays, and see a little more of the world.

With typical business acumen, Francis Frith foresaw that these new tourists would enjoy having souvenirs to commemorate their days out. For the next thirty years he travelled the country by train and by pony and trap, producing fine photographs of seaside resorts and beauty spots that were keenly bought by millions of Victorians. These prints were painstakingly pasted into family albums and pored over during the dark nights of winter, rekindling precious memories of summer excursions. Frith's studio was soon supplying retail shops all over the country, and by 1890 F Frith & Co had become the greatest specialist photographic publishing company in the world, with over 2,000 sales outlets, and pioneered the picture postcard.

FRANCIS FRITH'S LEGACY

Francis Frith had died in 1898 at his villa in Cannes, his great project still growing. By 1970 the archive he created contained over a third of a million pictures showing 7,000 British towns and villages.

Frith's legacy to us today is of immense significance and value, for the magnificent archive of evocative photographs he created provides a unique record of change in the cities, towns and villages throughout Britain over a century and more. Frith and his fellow studio photographers revisited locations many times down the years to update their views, compiling for us an enthralling and colourful pageant of British life and character.

We are fortunate that Frith was dedicated to recording the minutiae of everyday life. For it is this sheer wealth of visual data, the painstaking chronicle of changes in dress, transport, street layouts, buildings, housing and landscape that captivates us so much today, offering us a powerful link with the past and with the lives of our ancestors.

Computers have now made it possible for Frith's many thousands of images to be accessed almost instantly. The archive offers every one of us an opportunity to examine the places where we and our families have lived and worked down the years. Its images, depicting our shared past, are now bringing pleasure and enlightenment to millions around the world a century and more after his death.

For further information visit: www.francisfrith.com

INTERIOR DECORATION

Frith's photographs can be seen framed and as giant wall murals in thousands of pubs, restaurants, hotels, banks, retail stores and other public buildings throughout Britain. These provide interesting and attractive décor, generating strong local interest and acting as a powerful reminder of gentler days in our increasingly busy and frenetic world.

FRITH PRODUCTS

All Frith photographs are available as prints and posters in a variety of different sizes and styles. In the UK we also offer a range of other gift and stationery products illustrated with Frith photographs, although many of these are not available for delivery outside the UK – see our web site for more information on the products available for delivery in your country.

THE INTERNET

Over 100,000 photographs of Britain can be viewed and purchased on the Frith web site. The web site also includes memories and reminiscences contributed by our customers, who have personal knowledge of localities and of the people and properties depicted in Frith photographs. If you wish to learn more about a specific town or village you may find these reminiscences fascinating to browse. Why not add your own comments if you think they would be of interest to others? See **www.francisfrith.com**

PLEASE HELP US BRING FRITH'S PHOTOGRAPHS TO LIFE

Our authors do their best to recount the history of the places they write about. They give insights into how particular towns and villages developed, they describe the architecture of streets and buildings, and they discuss the lives of famous people who lived there. But however knowledgeable our authors are, the story they tell is necessarily incomplete.